A Rookie reader®

‖‖‖‖‖‖‖‖‖‖‖‖‖‖‖
W9-CPF-118 ARY
1177 N. MAIN
CRETE, IL 60417
708/ 672-8017

Going to Grandma's Farm

Written by Betsy Franco
Illustrated by Claudia Rueda

Children's Press®
A Division of Scholastic Inc.
New York • Toronto • London • Auckland • Sydney
Mexico City • New Delhi • Hong Kong
Danbury, Connecticut

CH
FRA
READER
C.1

For Grandma Mitz
—B.F.

To my husband Jorge, for always believing
—C.R.

Reading Consultants
Linda Cornwell
Literacy Specialist

Katharine A. Kane
Education Consultant
(Retired, San Diego County Office of Education
and San Diego State University)

Library of Congress Cataloging-in-Publication Data
Franco, Betsy.
  Going to Grandma's farm / written by Betsy Franco ; illustrated by
Claudia Rueda.
        p. cm. – (Rookie reader)
Summary: A family from the city uses various modes of transportation as
they travel to visit their grandmother on her farm.
  ISBN 0-516-22875-7 (lib. bdg.)   0-516-27787-1 (pbk.)
  [1. Transportation–Fiction. 2. Travel–Fiction. 3.
Grandmothers–Fiction. 4. Farm life–Fiction.] I. Rueda, Claudia, ill.
II. Title. III. Series.
  PZ7.F8475 Go 2003
  [E]–dc21

                                        2002015594

© 2003 by Betsy Franco
Illustrations © 2003 by Claudia Rueda
All rights reserved. Published simultaneously in Canada.
Printed in the United States of America.

CHILDREN'S PRESS, and A ROOKIE READER®, and associated logos are
trademarks and or registered trademarks of Grolier Publishing Co., Inc.
SCHOLASTIC and associated logos are trademarks and or registered
trademarks of Scholastic Inc.
1 2 3 4 5 6 7 8 9 10 R 12 11 10 09 08 07 06 05 04 03

We're going to our grandma's farm.

We ride in a cab.

We ride in a plane.

We ride on a boat.

We ride on a train.

We see Grandma!

We ride in her jeep.

Watch out for the sheep.

Beep! Beep! Beep!

Now we're all at
Grandma's farm.

We ride the horses
from the barn!

Word List (31 words)

a	Grandma	ride
all	grandma's	see
at	her	sheep
barn	horses	the
beep	in	to
boat	jeep	train
cab	now	watch
farm	on	we
for	our	we're
from	out	
going	plane	

About the Author

Betsy Franco lives in Palo Alto, California, where she has written more than forty books for children, including picture books, poetry, and nonfiction. Her family includes her husband Doug, her three sons (who give her lots of story ideas), and her two cats. She starts writing very early in the morning when everyone but the cats are asleep.

About the Illustrator

Claudia Rueda was born in Bogota, Colombia, and lived there all her childhood. She moved to the United States five years ago with her husband. She has two little girls. She has written and illustrated several educational books published in South America and has also illustrated a children's book in Spain.